Drawing and Paintings
Poetry

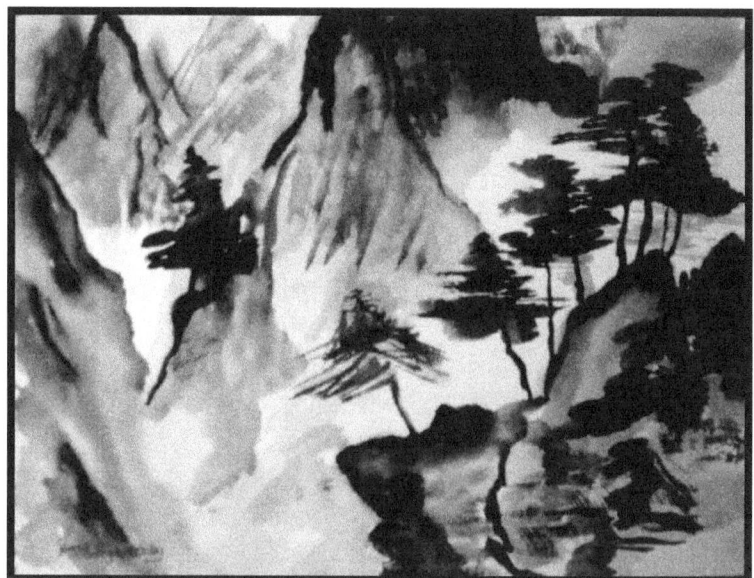

Peggy Leyva Conley

Thank you for reading in the event that you
Appreciate this book, please consider sharing the
Good words by leaving a review, or connect with
the author.

All rights reserved. Aside from brief quotations for
Media coverage and reviews, no part of this book
may be reproduced or distributed in any form
without the author's permission. Thank you for
supporting authors and a diverse, creative culture
by purchasing this book and complying with
copyright laws.

Copyright © 2016 - Peggy Leyva-Conley
Drawing and Paintings - Poetry

All Rights Reserved

Printed in the United States of America

ISBN-13: 978-1530939572 (Createspace) paperback
ISBN-10: 1530939577
BISAC: Art/Mixed Media

Table of Contents

About the Author
Forward
Themes
Huangshan Mountain Range
Forest Trees in the Woods
Yellow Mountains of China
Hanham Court in England
American Quarter Horses
Cliffs on the Pacific Coastline
Castle Villages of France
Valley of Animals
Mountain Rocks and Maples
Ocean Waves and Foam
Parish Archway
Winter Starkness
Peaceful River
Temples
Weeping Willow
The English Rectory
Sisters with Flowers in their Hair
Autumn
Aquila the Native Horse
Moon and Dusk
Teapot and Green Tea
Cherry Blossoms
Wild Bamboo
Tropical Plants and Lava Rock
Flower Blossoms
Rabbit

About the Author

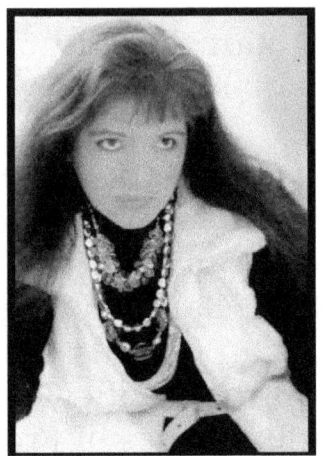

Artist and Poet Peggy Leyva Conley was born in
Hollister, California on the Pacific Central Coastal
Region of San Benito County bordering Monterey County.
She has resided in Hendersonville, Tennessee,
Old Hickory Lake a suburb of Nashville. She currently
resides in Rocklin, California on the bottom basin of
Tahoe National Forest near Capitol City of Sacramento.

At an early age she began Drawing and Painting.
This included writing Poetry, Theater Plays,
Storytelling, Photography, Ceramics, Woodworks,
and creating Music as forms of expression.

Mediums include working with Acrylics, Oils,
Watercolors, Pastels, Charcoal, Graphite, Pencil,
India Ink and mixed media.

The Artist has shown and Exhibited works Nationally
in parts of California, Tennessee and Washington DC.

Her works have also been shown Internationally
and sold in Private collections.

She has received the San Benito Artist high
Merit Award Scholarship in Hollister, California.

She has Won at Art exhibits Ribbon and Certificate Awards
throughout the years for her Artwork, and Ceramics.
This includes Poetry Awards at International events
held in San Francisco, California.

Memberships:

Hollister Art League, Hollister, California
Santa Cruz Poetry Association, Santa Cruz, California
Monthaven Art Society, Hendersonville, Tennessee
Plein Air Painters, Hendersonville, Tennessee
Untitled Artist, Nashville, Tennessee

National League American Pen Women-Nashville Branch
of (Artist, Writers, Musicians) in Tennessee
affiliated with Headquarters, Washington DC.

United Poets Laureate International – United Nations.

Order of St. Thomas of Acre, Victoria, Australia - Dame.

The Artist is also an International Musician and Published
Genealogist in Hardback books, Periodicals, and Newsletters.

Forward

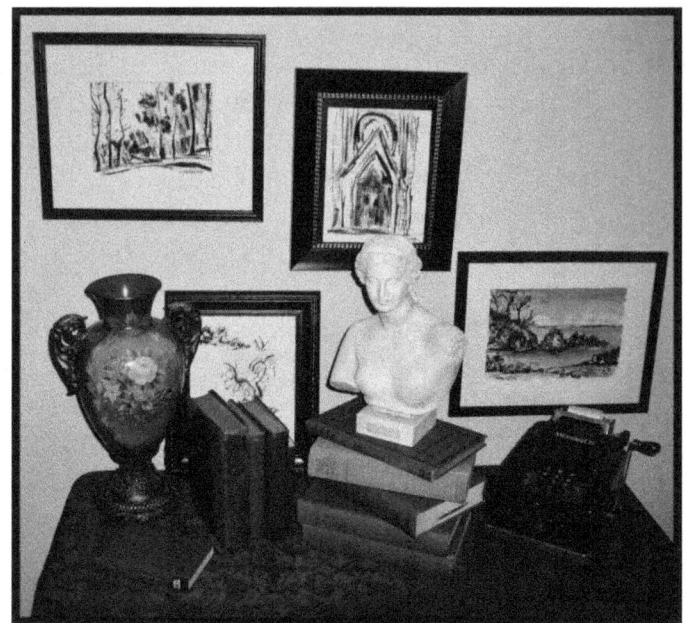

The Artist has created Artwork over the years
in her Art Studio and outdoors as a Plein Air
Painter on Traveling excursions across the
United States.

The selected Artworks shared in this book are in
Black and White showing the depth of expression.

Mediums

Acrylics, Pastels, Watercolors,
Charcoal, Pencil and India Ink.

Themes

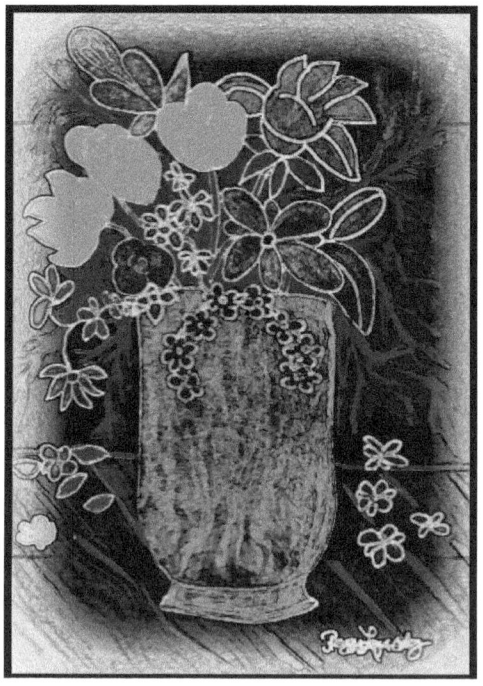

The Artwork and Poetry works include Themes
surrounding Nature, and Landscape scenes.

The environments such as Mountains, Trees,
Plants, Flowers, Ocean, Lakes, Streams, Animals,
People and structures are important in the settings.

Huangshan Mountain Range
Southern Anhui Province in Eastern China

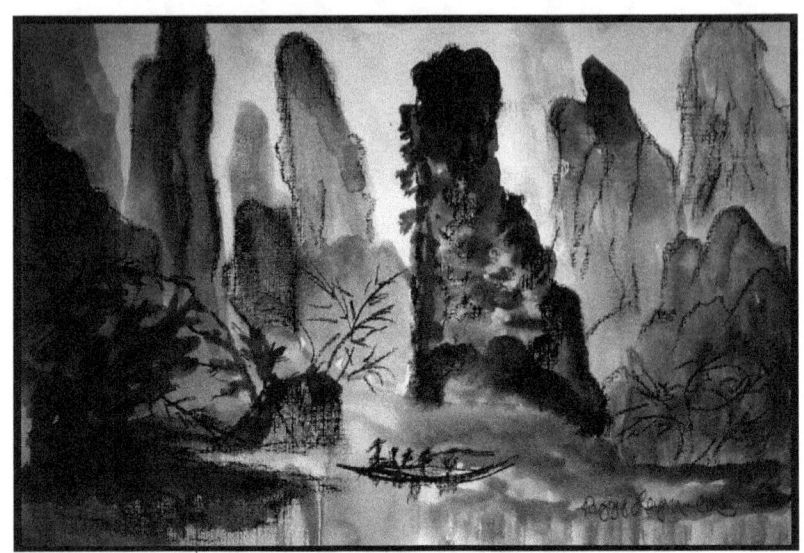

Watercolors – Pencil - India Ink
Mixed Media

Clear lake with Shadows
Canoe
Silence
Stillness
Early Morning
Tall Mountains Hoover
over the Valley below.

Forest Trees in the Woods

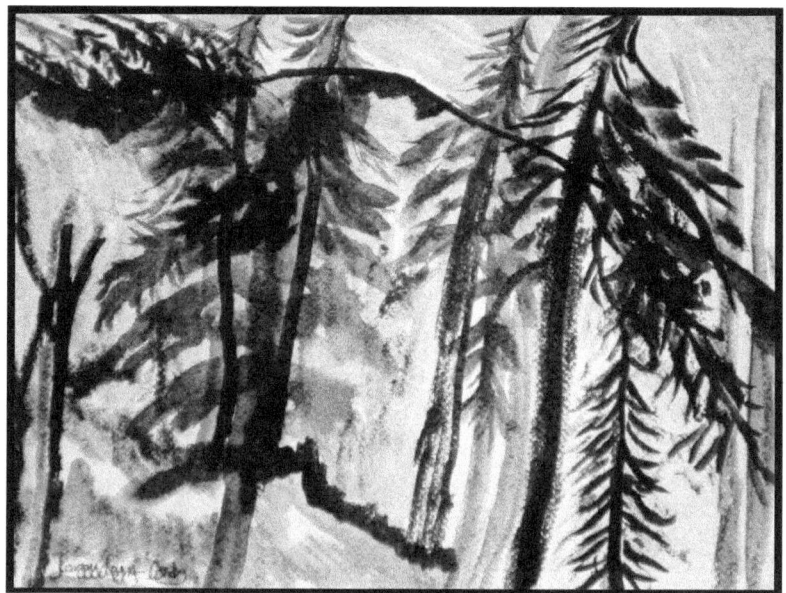

Watercolors

Timber Trees
Tilted
Mountain Side
Pine Leaves
Dusk Time
As Birds, fly away high
up above in the Sky.

Yellow Mountains of China

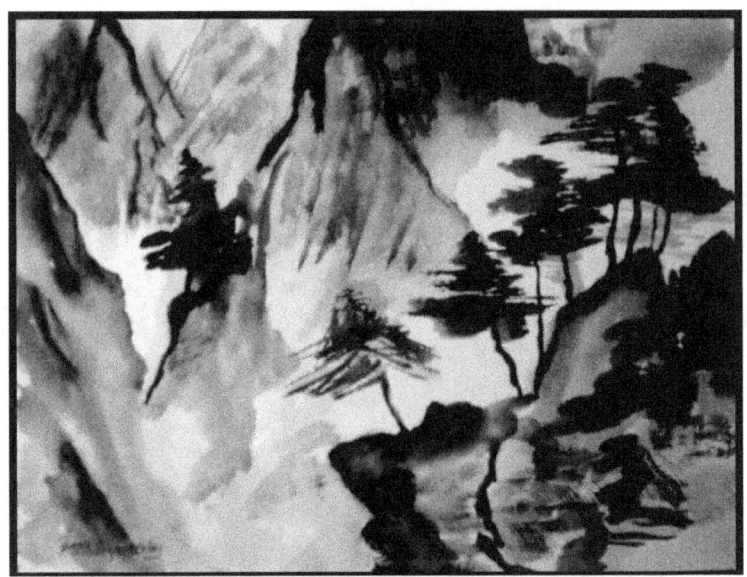

Watercolors

Tall Peaks
Shaped Rocks
Sea of Clouds
Temples hidden in Vallies below
Huangshan
Natural Wonder of the Earth
Beauty
a Paradise of Magic.

Hanham Court in England

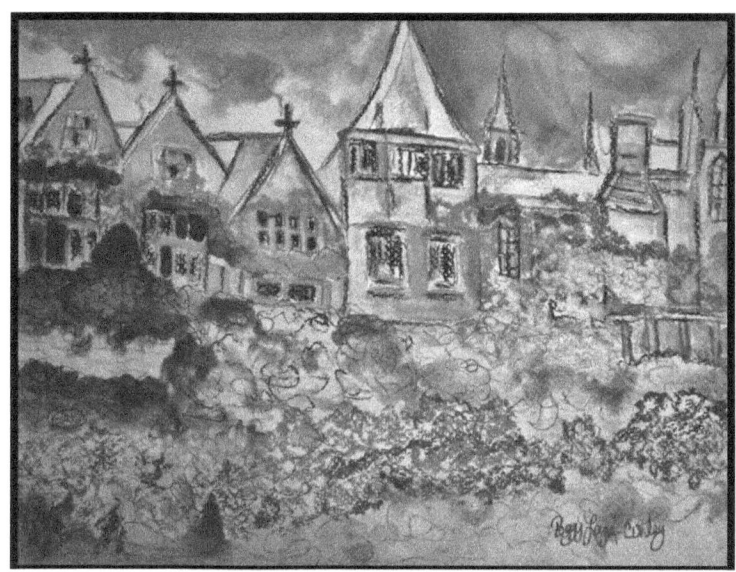

Watercolors – Drawing

Garden Flowers
Window Panes
Holy Crosses
Silence
Prayer
Morning Thoughts
of good Nature.
Antique Books
Tea
English Biscuits
Parlor Clock Chiming
Cat sleeping on Sofa

American Quarter Horses

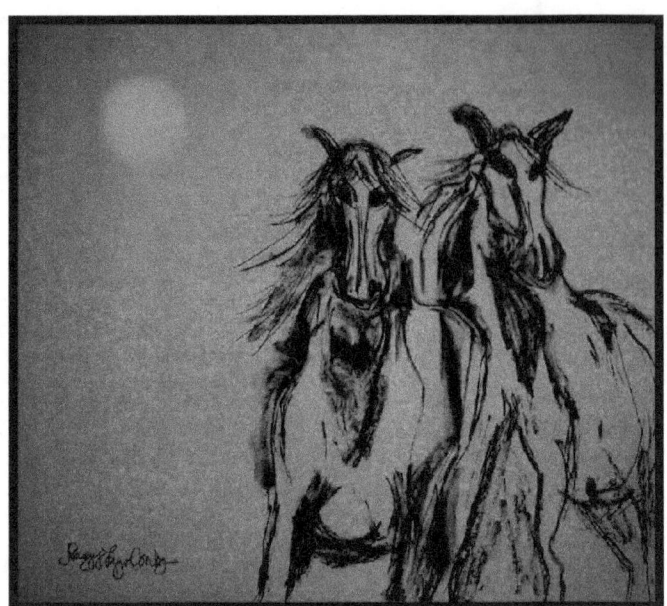

Charcoal - Drawing

Open up the Door
Unlock the Gate
Run
Gallop and Trout
Far away, up to the Hillside
where the Pretty Flowers
are in Bloom on a Warm
Summers day.

Cliffs on the Pacific Coastline

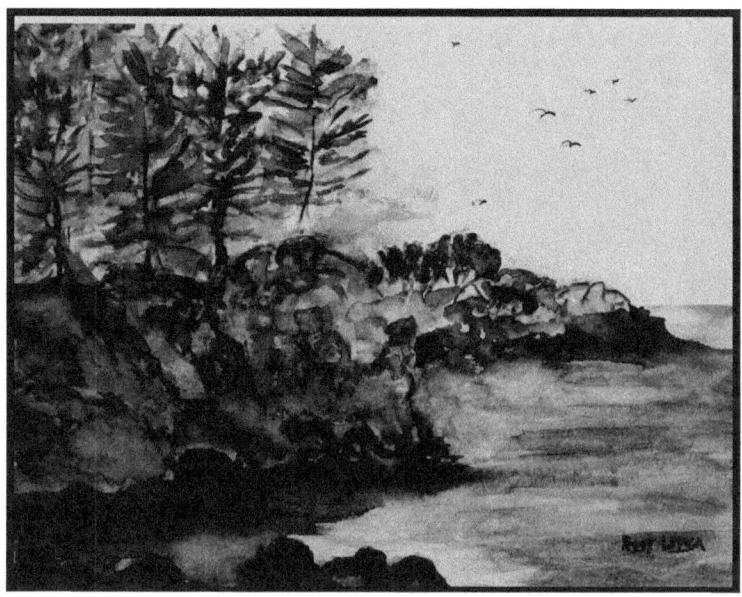

Watercolors

Carmel, California
It is a cool morning while out for a Walk.
Cliffs on the Pacific Coastline
are in stillness of a new day.
Seagulls fly on by looking
for Fish as nearby Fisherman
cast out their Nets from their
Boats in hopes of catching Halibut.

Castle Villages of France

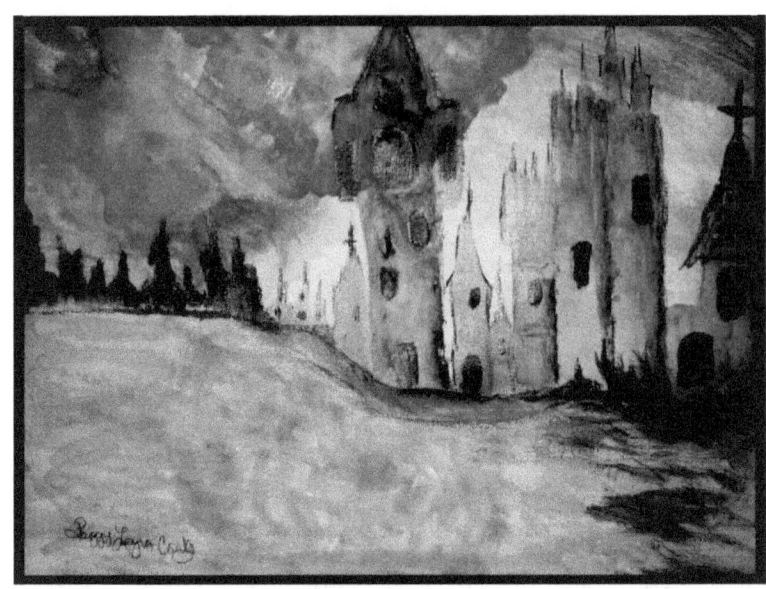

Watercolors

France
Distant Trees
Tall Towers
Windows
Cross
Morning
The Village
Sleeps.

Valley of Animals

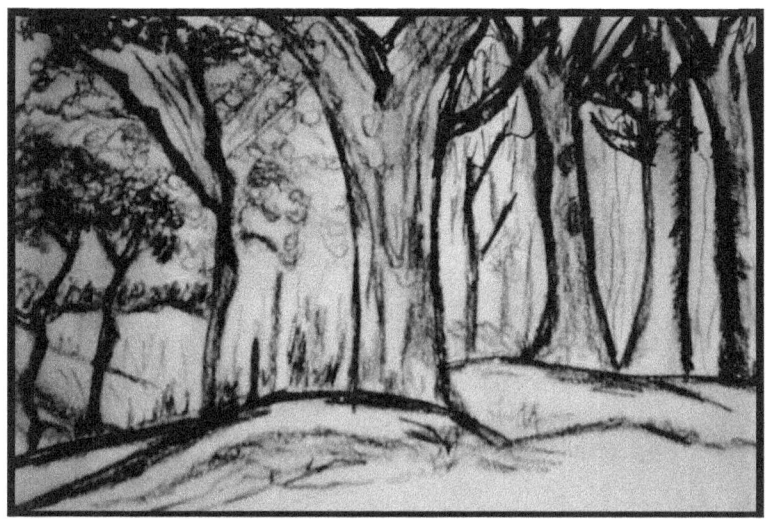

Charcoal

Deep and Dark Woods
Timber Land
Echoes of Wolfs are heard
along the paths.
Mountain Lions go in hiding.
Bear Cubs play on the hillside
as Ants crawl on the dirt road paths.
Caterpillars climb the trees and
Eagles hoover over their prey.

Mountain Rocks and Maples

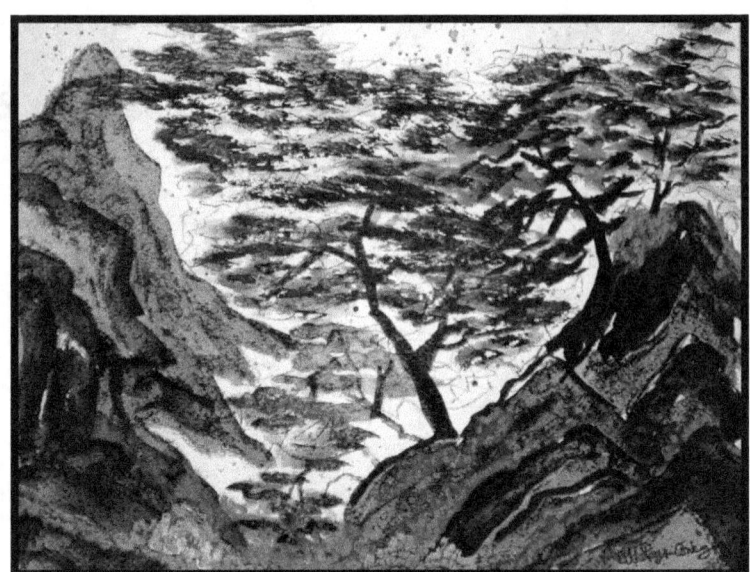

Acrylics – Watercolors
Mixed Media

Tall Mountain Peaks
Rocks
Maple Trees
Beauty.
Ancient men with walking Canes and
Elderly Women carrying baskets filled with breads.
The Children go running through the Valley below
Playing with Goats on the hillsides in May.

Ocean Waves and Foam

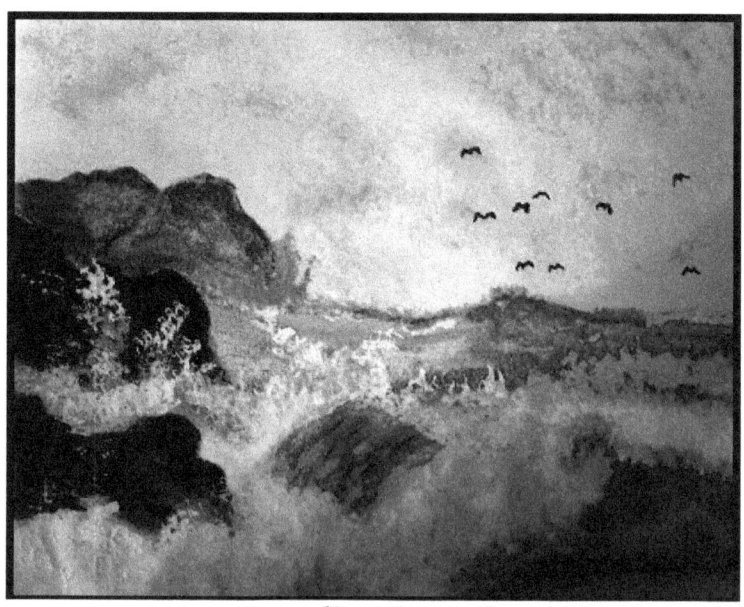

Acrylic - Pastels

Monterey, California
Ocean Waves come Crashing in
onto the Boulders and Rocks
with Sea Mist, and foam.
Seagulls are Flying
while heading in new
directions as evening has come.

Parish Archway

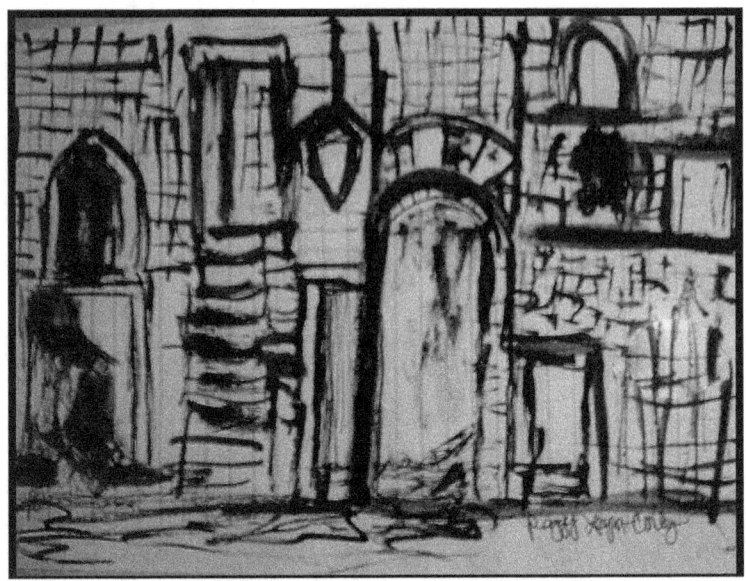

India-Ink – Drawing

Archway Passage.
Men in White and Black Robes
Prayer and Meditation
Candles Lit
Monk Music is chanted
Echoes down the Corridor
of Women running are heard.
One by one, the elderly Women sit
for Service and young girls try not to
Giggle to be lady like in the Parish.

Winter Starkness

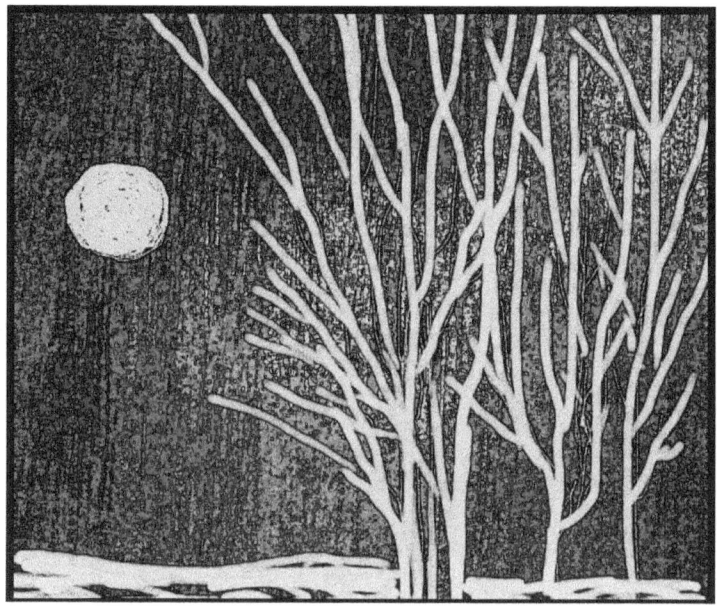

Drawing- Painting

Full Moon
Evening Sky
Snow on the
Stark Winter Trees.
Peaceful night
Owls Hooting
Deer eating frozen Raspberries
for their delight.

Peaceful River

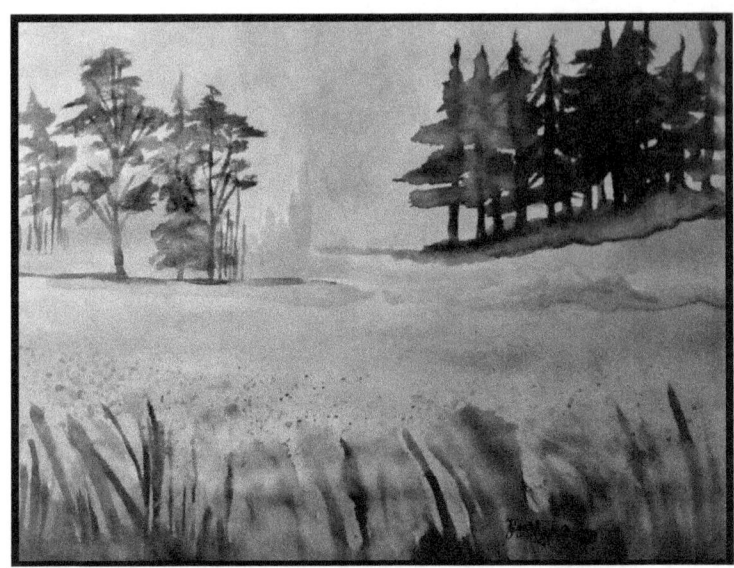

Watercolors

Pussy Willows
grow along the Shore banks
of a River in Wyoming.
Cattle Rustlers
come on in after work to join
others around an open Campfire
to participate in storytelling for the night.

Temples

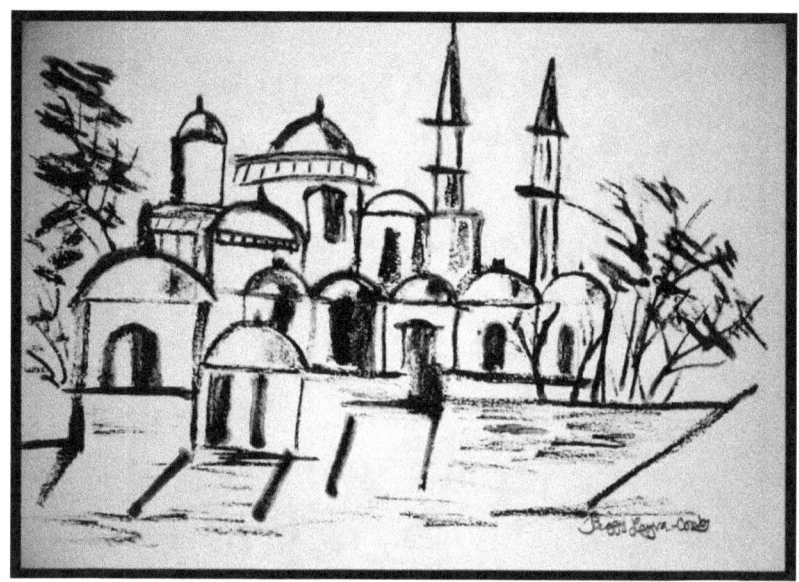

Charcoal

Desert Sands and
Temples all across
the lands.
Tambourines and
Guitar players
Join in on new Songs to sing.
Belly Dancers shake around their bodies
near the tables to perform
as men Clap and Dance in laughter
while drinking Red Port wine.

Weeping Willow

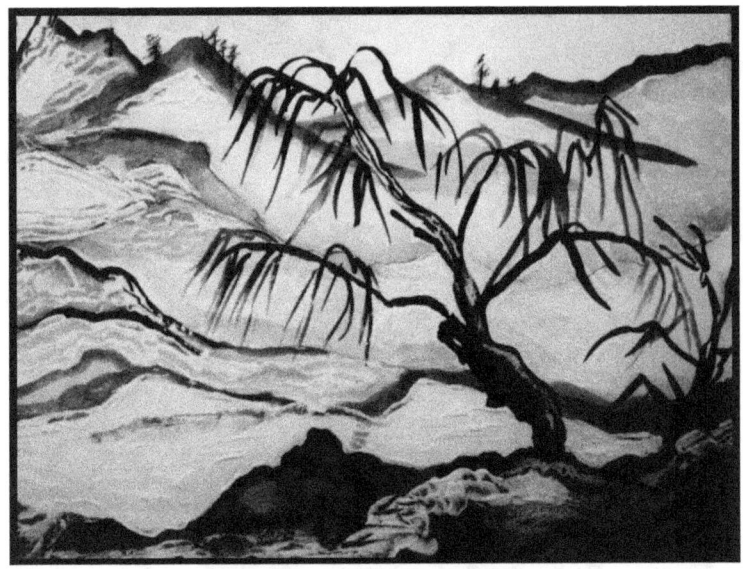

Acrylic – Watercolors

The Valley cries are heard from Wild Prey
making Howls from the Mountaintops
everywhere.
The endangered Wolves
are on the same list again as
years before for
Preservation of Animal life.
What must they do to
be heard out in the Wild?
other than to Cry late at night for peace.
Men with guns come
up in Jeeps looking
for big game to hunt during the
Season where Deer are in the
hundreds to thin out.

The Wild Wolves run with their
Packs for safety measures
to be undefeated.

Twenty or so go running into nearby
Caves for protection not to be seen
until danger is gone from their
Territory.

The Weeping Willow stands alone
Crying for the land and Animals which
feel defeated generation after generation.

The English Rectory

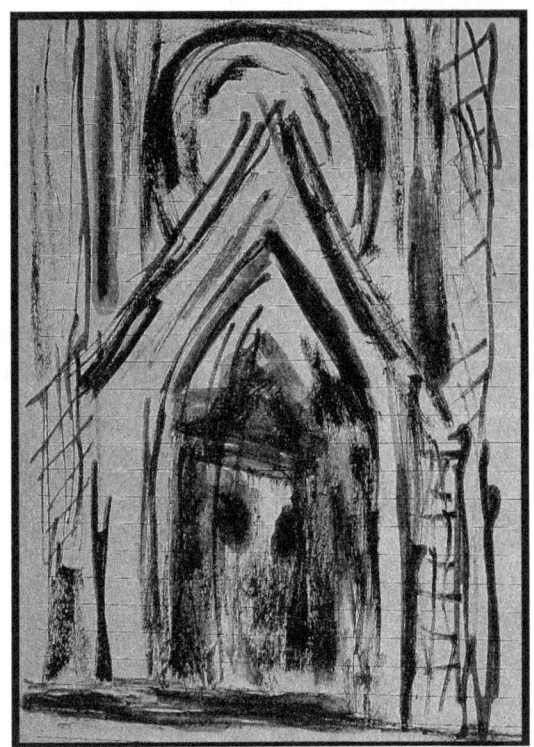

Charcoal - Black India Ink

May your doors be open to the
Orphans who have no place to live.

Early morning the English Rectory
opens their front Arch style doorways for
those on the streets looking for a bowl of
Soup and Bread to eat.

The retired Nurses come to put
in their days of work to give to the needy
a free health checkup and to help the Children
who are housed there.

The English Village has
those who come and bring
Bicycles for the children to ride
at the nearby park on
Summer School breaks.

Mothers in town bring
Homemade Chicken Pot Pies,
Apple and Cherry Croissants,
and warm Milk to feed all
the English Rectory.

It is a blessing for
all the children
to experience much love
given from those who care.

Sisters with Flowers in their Hair

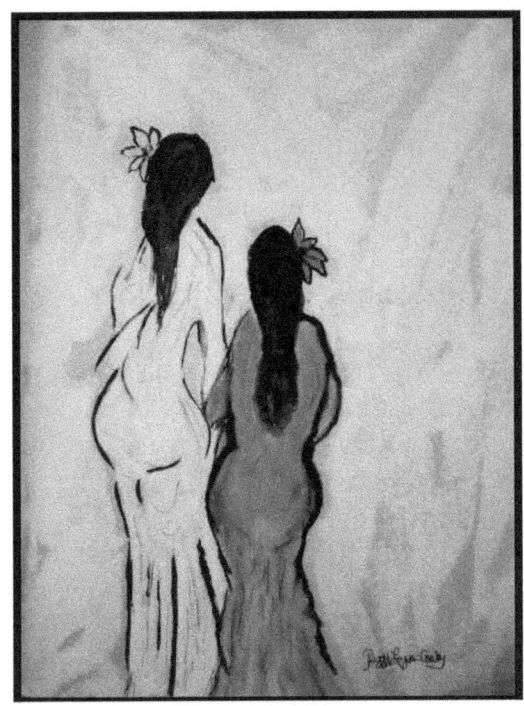

Watercolors

Walking a Path in Life
two Sisters hold each other's hands.
They pray for Peace and Joy
from the goodness of their Hearts.

The Journey in Life is a great reward
when there is someone to share
the Walk with and grow together
in the blessings given upon the earth.

Autumn

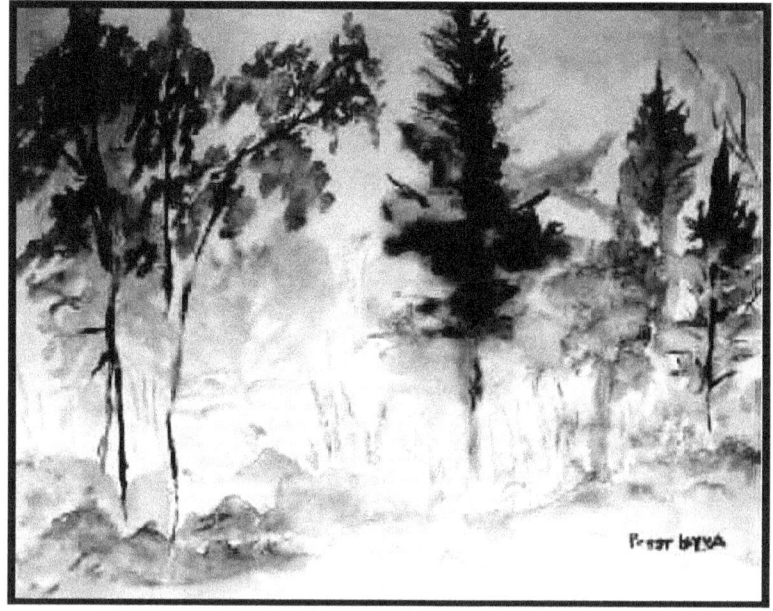

Watercolors

Autumn leaves of beautiful Colors with
Wooded Trees surrounding the Boulders and Rocks.

It is a Warm day with a cool gentle breeze
as one walks along the dirt road paths.

The Woodpeckers and Humming birds,
and the Crickets make sounds along the Riverbed.

At Nightfall the area is filled with Fireflies that light
up the Forest with magical wonder.

Aquila the Native Horse

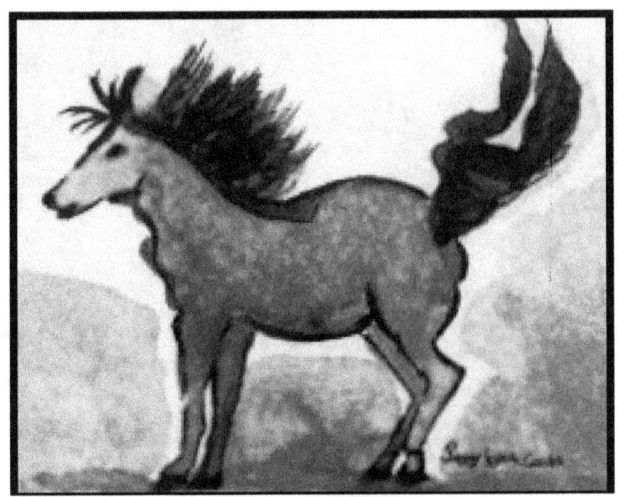

Watercolors

Run for Miles
Jump as high as you can
and Leap forward.

Aquila the Horse is as
Strong as could be, and
Smart on his Feet.
A Winner,
A Survivor,
and a Horse at Peace
on Native Cherokee land.

Moon and Dusk

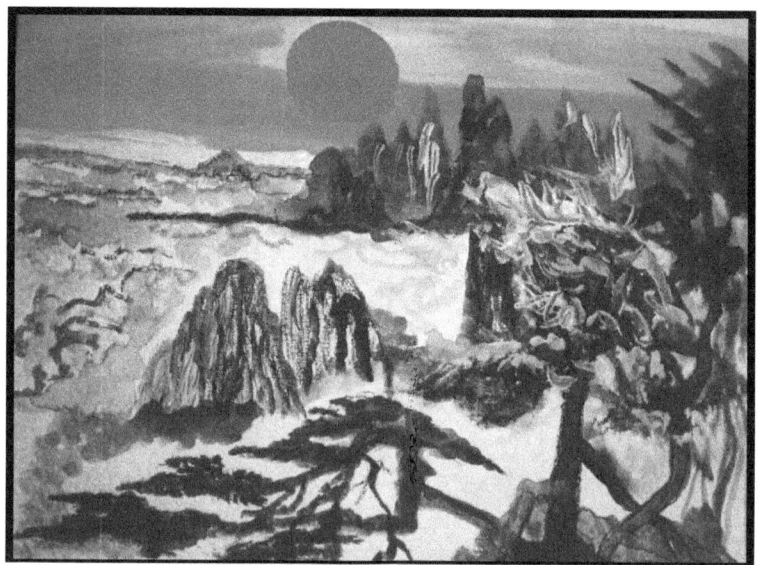

Acrylic – Charcoal – India Ink
Mixed Media

Full Moon and Jagged Mountaintops.
A Valley below with Cypress and Maple Trees
and Rivers that Flow down Stream.
Many explorers come into the Valley to study
the Birds, Lions, Deer, Monkeys
Snakes, Owls, Lady Bugs, Worms
Moths and Butterflies.
The Eco System replenishes itself
as part of Nature in purity.

Teapot and Green Tea

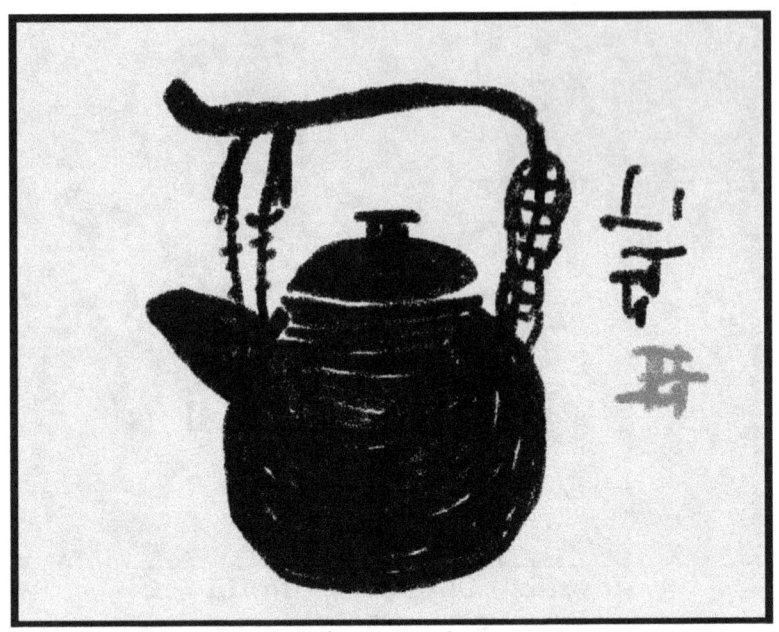

Ink Drawing

Green Tea
Meditation
Morning Reading glasses
Newspaper
Cats
Walk to Mailbox
Take morning brisk Walk
Hear the Birds Sing and Chirp
Play Classical Music
throughout the house.
Paint in the afternoon lovely field of Flowers.
Pray for the blessings in Life.

Cherry Blossoms

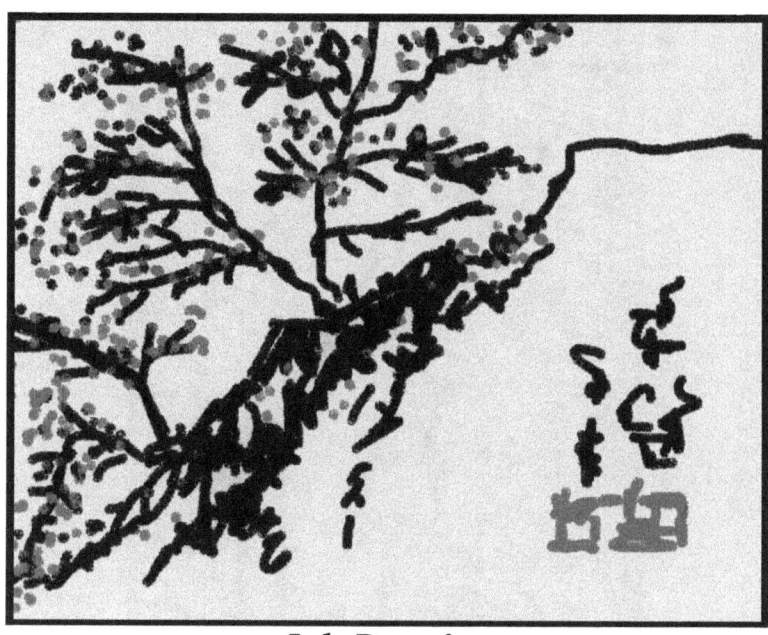

Ink Drawing

Mountain of Cherry Trees
Have Blossoms in full bloom.
A place of tranquilly and Beauty.
Enchanting and mesmerizing.
Village people sleep in Cabins
and restless Dogs go running to watch
the Goats climb the hillside
in the late afternoon.

Wild Bamboo

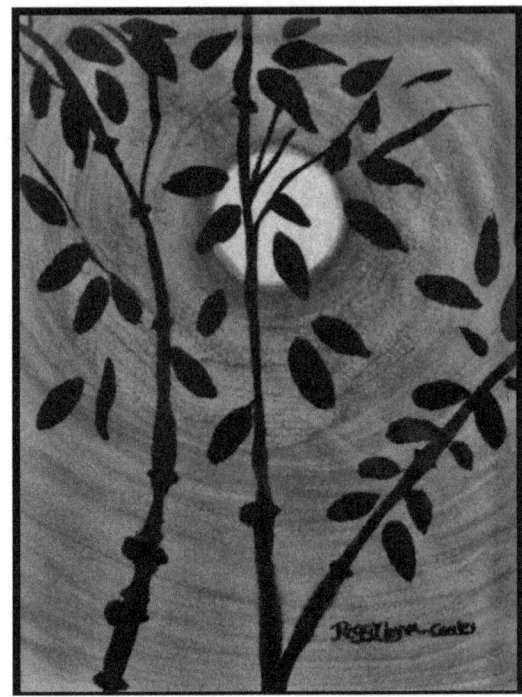

Watercolors - Pastels

The Moon has risen so bright tonight
above the Sky so high.
Stargazing is a thing of Joy and delight.
Wild Bamboo sticks are a Natural
and magnificent beauty.
Scent of Wild Mint growing in the
Garden is rather becoming.
Cactus plants in round Clay Pots
are treasures to enjoy.
Azaleas are in abundance.
Red and Pink Roses are in bloom.
It is a place of warmth and peace.

Tropical Plants and Lava Rock

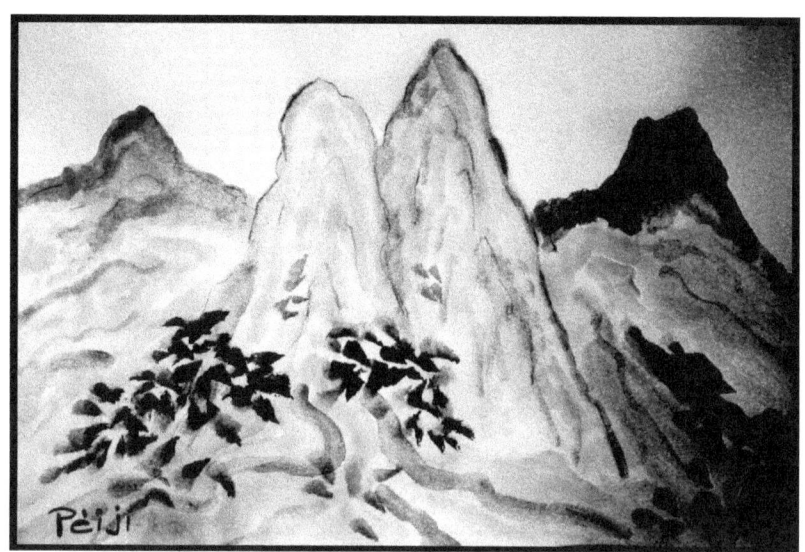

Watercolors

Black Lava Rock
Formations
Tall
New Life
Plants of every kind
fill the Valley

Tall Mountains
Stand in the center like two lovers
as they Kiss and unite as one.

Flower Blossoms

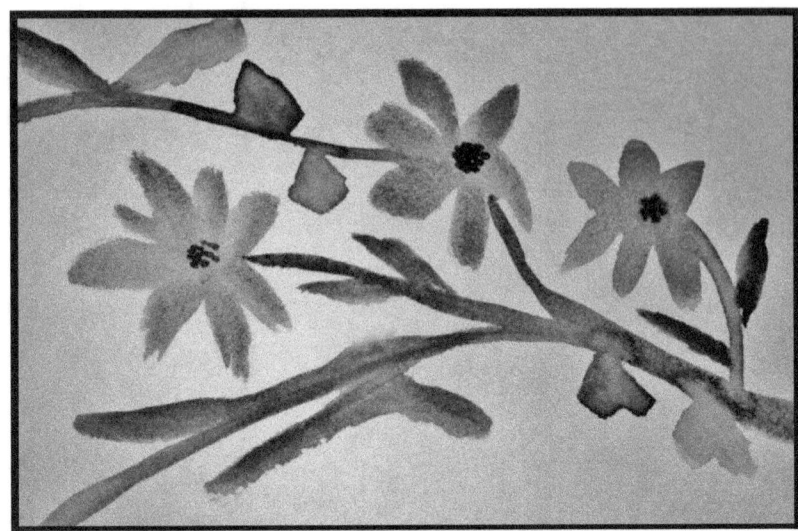

Watercolors

Flower Blossoms
Vines
Strength
Long
Beauty
Scent of Heavenly delight.
Nature
Stillness

Rabbit

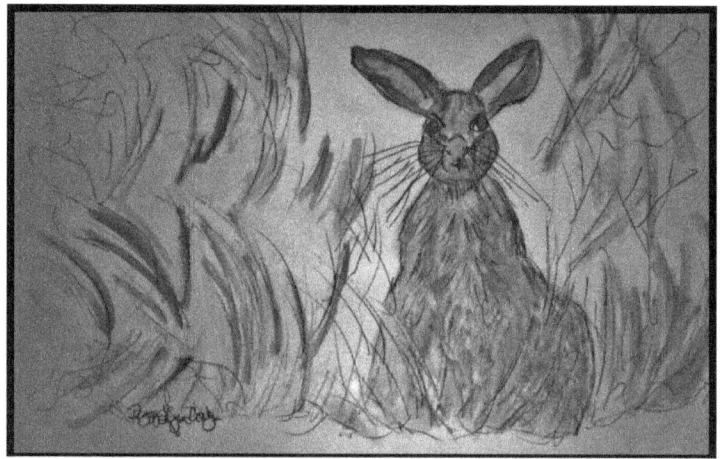

Charcoal – Pencil

In the green Grass swaying
on a windy day a Rabbit
came out from hiding
and just stared.

Normally there was a group of
them hiding under the house
that would come on out if the
area was clear from ones two Orange
Tabby Cats named
BoBo and Boots.

Yes, ones Joy in Life!

It was out on a place called
Old Hickory Lake while one was
outdoors for the day.

It is a haven out with nature.

A place the Squirrels looked for
Acorns and the Possums came up onto
the backyard Patio each day looking for food.

A place Wild Deer come up and ate from the
Wild Flowers, and sat under the Apple trees.

A place that once belonged to the Cherokee
Indian Nation as Sacred Hunting ground.

A place of Blue Herons sitting on
Wooden Logs along the Lakes shore.

A place the Red Robins, Yellow Sparrows,
and Bluejays would come around to sing a Song
or to Chirp in the Red Berry trees.

A place where one would sit out in the front
yard on a Chair and Cast Iron Table to
Write or Paint in drawing books during
Summer days.

A place of magical dreams where music and poetry
was created back in Tennessee.

A place one will always Treasure forever
for the love of Nature and beauty.

Literary Published Works
Peggy Leyva Conley

Books

Drawing and Paintings
with Poetry – Published 2016

Winter Season with Nature – Landscape Scenes
Poetry and Photography - Published 2016

Life in the Country – White Cotton Sheets
Poetry and Photography – Published 2016

At the Heart of Aromatherapy – Nature Botanicals
Herbs – Soaps – Oils – Fragrance – Published 2016

The Transcendental Zen Garden
Poetry and Photography – Published 2016

Poetic Inspirations
Poetry and Photography – Published 2016

Discography - Music

Passages of Time
(Classical: Film Music) - Released 2010

Canterbury Manor
(Classical: Chamber Music) – Released 2013

Ancient Garden of Knowledge
(Classical: Orchestral) – Released 2013

Midnight Telephone Blues
(Blues: Delta Style) - Released 2013

In the Face of Blues
(Acoustic Blues) – Released 2013

Mountain Blues
(Acoustic Blues) – Released 2013

Available on International Distribution

www.ingramcontent.com/pod-product-compliance
Lightning Source LLC
Chambersburg PA
CBHW080644190526
45169CB00009B/3497